The American Girls
Quiz Book

Published by Pleasant Company Publications

Visit our Web site at **americangirl.com**.

Printed in China.
05 06 07 08 09 10 C&C 10 9 8 7 6 5 4 3 2

Questions or comments?
Call 1-800-845-0005, visit **americangirl.com**, or write to:
American Girl, P.O. Box 620497, Middleton, WI 53562-0497.

Editorial development by Jennifer Hirsch
Art directed and designed by Cesca Piuma
Produced by Paula Moon-Bailey, Virginia Gunderson,
Judith Lary, and Dana Hoberg
Illustrations by Dan Andreasen, Nick Backes, Bill Farnsworth,
Renée Graef, Susan McAliley, Susan Moore, Lisa Pfeiffer, John Pugh,
Walter Rane, Dahl Taylor, Jean-Paul Tibbles, and Mike Wimmer
Historical research by Mark Speltz and Sally Wood

Table of Contents

Who's Who

Which American Girl Is Most Like You?

Circle the answers that best match your own life. Then put a mark beside the signatures below for each American Girl listed after your answer.

Addy _____   Josefina _____   Kaya _____   Kirsten _____

Molly _____   Samantha _____   Kit _____   Felicity _____

1. In my family,

a. I am an only child. (Samantha)

b. I have one or two siblings. (Felicity, Addy, Kit)

c. I have three or four siblings. (Kaya, Josefina, Kirsten, Molly)

2. My favorite animal is a

a. horse. (Felicity, Kaya)

b. dog. (Kit, Molly, Samantha)

c. baby animal of any kind. (Kirsten, Josefina)

3. My family handles money

a. with care, and sometimes there's not enough for things I'd like. (Josefina, Addy, Kirsten, Kit)

b. as if we have plenty for all our needs and wants. (Felicity, Samantha)

4. In the summer, I usually

a. try to earn some money. (Addy, Kit, Kirsten, Josefina)

b. travel with my family. (Kaya)

c. go to camp on my own. (Molly)

d. stay at a vacation home or cabin with my family. (Samantha)

e. visit my grandparents. (Felicity)

5. **One of my best qualities is that I**

    a. am a great team player. (Kit, Molly)

    b. try hard to do well in school. (Kirsten, Addy)

    c. am not easily intimidated. (Felicity)

    d. get along well with everyone in my family. (Josefina)

    e. stay true to my friends, no matter what others say. (Samantha)

    f. don't give up until I've reached my goal. (Kaya)

6. **But I admit that I have been known to**

    a. get impatient. (Felicity)

    b. boast or brag. (Kaya)

    c. squabble with my siblings. (Molly)

    d. imagine running away and joining another family. (Kirsten)

    e. leave a good friend to be with a more popular girl. (Addy)

    f. be gloomy about changes instead of looking on the bright side. (Kit)

7. **People say that I am**

    a. courageous. (Kaya, Addy)

    b. spunky. (Felicity)

    c. imaginative. (Molly, Kit)

    d. hardworking. (Kirsten)

    e. kind. (Josefina, Samantha)

8. **I hope someday I get the chance to**

    a. perform onstage. (Molly)

    b. write for the newspaper. (Kit)

    c. help people who are less fortunate than I am. (Samantha)

    d. become an expert horsewoman. (Kaya)

    e. work for a cause I believe in. (Felicity)

Scoring

If you have a lot of marks beside one name, read about your "twin" below to see how you're alike! If you have several marks beside a variety of names, then read about those American Girls to find out what you have in common.

If you're like Kaya . . .

You probably live in a large family, and you love horses. Kaya was an excellent rider, although boasting about her horse got her into trouble! Like Kaya, you may face great challenges in your life—and use bravery and determination to solve them.

If you're like Felicity . . .

You're a free spirit who likes to be in the middle of the action! Felicity preferred horseback riding and high adventure to fussy, "sitting down" activities such as sewing. She wasn't afraid to stand up to bullies or wrongdoers, and neither are you.

If you're like Josefina . . .

You're sensitive and love babies—especially baby animals! Josefina wanted to be a healer. She raised an orphaned newborn goat by hand. When her sisters argued, Josefina tried to make peace. Like Josefina, you are the peacemaker in your family.

If you're like Kirsten . . .

You adore kittens, puppies, anything small and furry—you'd even take in a baby raccoon, as Kirsten did. Although you love your family and work hard at school and at home, you sometimes can't help wondering what it might be like to live in a different family!

If you're like Addy . . .

You're responsible with money, and you're a top-notch student. At school, Addy studied hard and won the spelling bee. She also learned about the pitfalls of popularity—and what it takes to be a true friend. Like Addy, you're brave and set high standards for yourself.

If you're like Samantha . . .

You're not afraid to go against the grain. Samantha befriended Nellie, a servant girl, and took great risks to help her friend, despite the disapproval of others. Samantha knew it's not how a person looks on the outside but what's inside that matters, and so do you.

If you're like Kit . . .

You're thrifty and you love dogs, but you're not crazy about big changes. When Kit had to move her bedroom into the attic, she was upset at first. Once she stopped moping, she found the attic actually made a pretty cool room! Like Kit, you tackle problems head-on.

If you're like Molly . . .

You enjoy daydreaming about your future—as a star! Molly loved her dance class and was thrilled to get the lead role. At home she sometimes teased her brother, but at school and at camp, she knew how to organize a winning team. For both you and Molly, your active imagination is your greatest asset.

Kaya 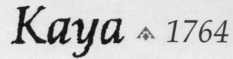 1764

1. **Kaya's full name was Kaya'aton'my'. What did her name mean? To find out, unscramble the letters:**

   SEH   HOW   RESARGAN   CORKS

2. **Kaya was a member of which Native American tribe?**

   a. Apache

   b. Cherokee

   c. Navajo

   d. Nez Perce

3. **According to Kaya, her twin brothers are "just the right age for mischief." How old does Kaya say they are?**

   a. three summers old

   b. four winters old

   c. twenty moons old

4. **Who's who? Draw lines to match the Kaya characters with their names:**

   Kaya's twin brothers   Brown Deer and Speaking Rain

   Kaya's sisters   Fox Tail and Raven

   Kaya's parents   Steps High and Sparks Flying

   two boys who bother Kaya   Toe-ta and Eetsa

   Kaya's horse and her foal   Wing Feather and Sparrow

6

5. **Kaya's land of white-peaked mountains, broad valleys, and winding rivers is now part of which states?**

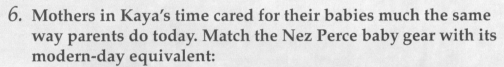

   a. Washington, Oregon, and Idaho

   b. North Dakota and South Dakota

   c. Maine, New Hampshire, and Vermont

6. **Mothers in Kaya's time cared for their babies much the same way parents do today. Match the Nez Perce baby gear with its modern-day equivalent:**

dried meat	baby carrier
cattail fluff	teething biscuit
medicine woman	disposable diapers
cradleboard	pediatrician

Nez Perce babies slept in buckskin cradles that hung from the ceiling like hammocks.

Felicity ❧ 1774

1. **In 1774, if you believed that America should stay under English rule, you were a**

        a. Patriot.   b. Loyalist.

2. **Match each person to his belief by putting an X below "Loyalist" or "Patriot." The first one has been done for you.**

	Patriot	*Loyalist*
Felicity's father	x	
Grandfather		
Elizabeth's father		
Ben		

3. **Who's who? Match each person to his or her position:**

Ben	shopkeeper
Father	plantation owner
Miss Manderly	tanner
Isaac	apprentice
Jiggy Nye	teacher
Grandfather	drummer in the militia

4. **True or false? Elizabeth and Annabelle were Felicity's best friends.**

5. Annabelle called Felicity's father a

    a. Patriot.

    b. Loyalist.

    c. traitor.

    d. hothead.

6. Felicity called Annabelle

    a. Tinkerbell.   b. Bananabelle.   c. Bluebell.

"Oh, my darling Ben," said Felicity in a high voice. She was pretending to be Annabelle— who was not amused!

Josefina ✳ 1824

1. **True or false? Josefina was named for a saint, San José.**

2. **Draw lines to match Josefina and her sisters to some of their characteristics:**

   Josefina   impatient, headstrong

   Clara   hopeful, timid

   Francisca   gentle, understanding

   Ana   practical, sensible

3. **True or false? Josefina and her family were citizens of Mexico.**

4. **True or false? Josefina's godmother, Tía Magdalena, was Mamá's sister.**

5. **Who's who? Match the names to the people in Josefina's world:**

   Teresita   Josefina's grandfather

   Abuelito   the doll Mamá had made

   Carmen   Tía Dolores's servant

   Patrick O'Toole   the cook on the rancho

   Mariana   the cook's husband

   Niña   an American scout

   Miguel   Josefina's friend, a Pueblo Indian

6. One of Tía Dolores's favorite sayings was

    a. "Haste makes waste."

    b. "A stitch in time saves nine."

    c. "The saints cry over lost time."

7. What were the names of Ana's two little boys? To find out, change each letter to the one that comes before it in the alphabet:

K V B O   B O U P O J P

Josefina and her grandmother, Abuelita, loved to play games with Ana's boys.

Kirsten ♥ 1854

1. **Kirsten's family came to America from**

    a. Sweden.

    b. Norway.

    c. Denmark.

2. **The Larsons were traveling to settle in which state? Unscramble the word to find out:**

    N I T O M E A N S

3. **During the long journey, Kirsten's friend Marta became very sick. Kirsten's parents did not want her to visit Marta, because they were afraid Kirsten might catch Marta's illness. What did Marta have?**

    a. measles

    b. cholera

    c. polio

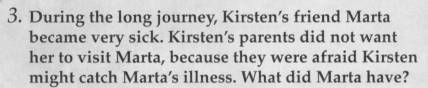

4. **Mama and Papa's favorite saying was "Don't lose _____."**

    a. hope

    b. your way

    c. heart

5. **True or false? When Kirsten missed her grandmother, Mormor, she looked at the sun.**

6. **Who's who? Match the names to the people in Kirsten's world:**

Anna and Lisbeth   Kirsten's brothers

Lars and Peter   Kirsten's teacher

Uncle Olav   Kirsten's secret friend

Miss Winston   Kirsten's baby sister

Mr. Berkhoff   Papa's brother

Singing Bird   Kirsten's cousins

Britta   a trapper

Old Jack   owner of the general store in Maryville

Addy ☀ 1864

1. Addy's name was short for *Aduke*, an African word that means

   a. truly brave.

   b. beautiful.

   c. much loved.

   d. strong.

2. Addy and Momma escaped from Master Stevens's plantation in North Carolina. They wanted to go to Philadelphia, where they could be free. To do that, they needed to travel

   a. north.

   b. south.

   c. east.

   d. west.

3. True or false? The night Addy and Momma escaped, Addy left her doll Janie with her baby sister, Esther.

4. Why did Addy name her new doll Ida Bean?

   a. Because she was as thin as a beanpole.

   b. Because she was stuffed with beans.

   c. Because Addy found her in a bean field.

5. **Who's where? Match the people and places in Addy's world:**

Auntie Lula   a lady who runs a safe house
                           on the Underground Railroad

Master Stevens   owner of a small dress shop in
                           Philadelphia

Sarah   the cruel plantation owner in
                           North Carolina

Miss Dunn   Mr. Golden's mother, who lives
                           at the boarding house

Mrs. Ford   the preacher at Trinity A.M.E.
                           Church

M'dear   the cook on the plantation in
                           North Carolina

Reverend Drake   Addy's teacher at Sixth Street
                           School

Miss Caroline   Addy's best friend in Philadelphia

6. **Addy posed a riddle: "What's smaller than
a dog but can put a bear on the run?"
Addy's brother, Sam, knew the answer.
Do you?**

Samantha 🐚 1904

1. **Who's who? Match the names to the characters in Samantha's world:**

Uncle Gard	Uncle Gard's lady friend, whom he marries
Jenny and Bridget	Samantha's friend, a servant girl
Agnes and Agatha	Grandmary's son
Elsa	Samantha's grandmother
Hawkins	Nellie's little sisters
Grandmary	Grandmary's butler
Cornelia	Cornelia's twin sisters
Nellie	Grandmary's grouchy maid

2. **True or false? Samantha was an orphan.**

3. **Grandmary had many strict opinions. Which of the following statements was *not* what Grandmary believed?**

   a. A young lady must not ask questions of her elders.

   b. Automobiles are dreadful, horrible machines.

   c. Voting is not a lady's concern.

   d. A lady does not earn money.

   e. Sledding is good, wholesome exercise.

   f. Babies are not a proper subject for young girls.

4. **True or false? Jessie, Grandmary's seamstress, left to become an actress.**

5. **What message was Samantha stitching on her sampler?**

   a. A Friend in Need Is a Friend Indeed.

   b. Faithful Friends Forever Be.

   c. Absence Makes the Heart Grow Fonder.

   d. Actions Speak Louder Than Words.

6. **What was the Admiral's pet name for Agnes and Agatha?**

   a. the Tiger Lilies   b. the Bobbsey Twins   c. two peas in a pod

Kit ❧ 1934

1. **Kit's real name was**
   a. Margaret Mildred Kittredge.
   b. Katherine Anne Kittredge.
   c. Charlotte Dorothy Kittredge.

2. **True or false? Kit loved the way Mother redecorated her bedroom in pale pink with white trim and lots of lace.**

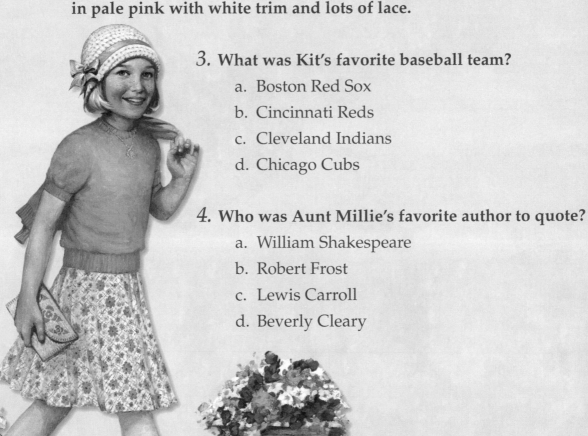

3. **What was Kit's favorite baseball team?**
   a. Boston Red Sox
   b. Cincinnati Reds
   c. Cleveland Indians
   d. Chicago Cubs

4. **Who was Aunt Millie's favorite author to quote?**
   a. William Shakespeare
   b. Robert Frost
   c. Lewis Carroll
   d. Beverly Cleary

5. When Mother got the idea to take in boarders, she called it a
_____. To find out what word she used, change each
letter to the one that comes before it in the alphabet:

CSBJOTUPSN

6. Who's who? Match each person to his or her description:

Stirling Howard	a hobo
Ruthie Smithens	the newspaper editor
Uncle Hendrick	Kit's brother
Will	a boarder at Kit's house
Gibb	Kit's best friend
Charlie	the thrifty woman who raised Dad
Aunt Millie	Mother's disapproving uncle

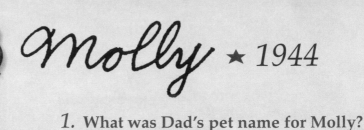

Molly ★ 1944

1. **What was Dad's pet name for Molly?**

    a. Molly Malone

    b. Olly Molly

    c. Ole Golly

2. **Molly grew up during**

    a. the Civil War.

    b. World War One.

    c. World War Two.

    d. the Korean War.

3. **Molly's father, Captain James McIntire, was a _____.**
For the answer, change each letter to the one that comes before it in the alphabet:

    E P D U P S

4. **Mrs. Gilford came to keep house for the McIntires because Molly's mother**

    a. went to work in an airplane factory.

    b. became an army nurse.

    c. went to work for the Red Cross.

5. When Molly, Linda, and Susan were trying to think up good Halloween costumes, Ricky offered some ideas. Which of the following was *not* one of Ricky's ideas?

   a. Cinderella and the two ugly stepsisters

   b. the Three Little Pigs

   c. the Three Bears

   d. the Three Stooges

6. Who's who? Match the names to the characters in Molly's world:

Emily Bennett	Molly's dance teacher
Mrs. Gilford	the English princesses
Miss Campbell	Molly's good friends
Miss LaVonda	the camp director
Linda and Susan	Molly's third-grade teacher
Elizabeth and Margaret Rose	a girl from England
Miss Butternut	the McIntires' housekeeper

Fabulous Fashions

Which of the American Girls would you want to dress like?

To find out, circle the answers that best express your feelings about clothes:

1.
   a. I like a full closet with plenty of clothes to pick from.
   b. As long as I have a few favorites to wear, that's fine.
   c. I wish I could wear my favorite outfit every single day.

2.
   a. I love wearing nice dresses or skirts and tops.
   b. I prefer to wear pants.
   c. I'm not fussy—I'll wear whatever, as long as I don't look weird in it.

3.
   a. I like stylish, dressy shoes and boots.
   b. I enjoy wearing casual, comfortable shoes, such as sneakers.
   c. My preferred footwear: sandals, flip-flops, or bare feet.

4.
   a. I love having my parents provide me with nice clothes.
   b. I like hand-me-downs. They're comfy—and they're free.
   c. It would be great if I could sew exactly the kind of clothes I like.

5. **In each of these groups, can you find the item that doesn't
   belong with the others?**

Clothing worn on your legs:	Clothing worn on your head:	Underwear:
bloomers	sunbonnet	sarape
breeches	boater	drawers
pattens	mob cap	shift
pantalettes	camisa	underpetticoat

6. **Draw lines to show which American Girl would have
   worn each item.**

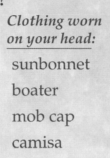

bloomers	Molly
mob cap	Kirsten
buckskin dress	Felicity
sarape	Samantha
feed-sack dress	Josefina
saddle shoes	Kaya
sunbonnet	Kit

23

1. **True or false? Felicity loved wearing stays.**

2. **In Felicity's day, people wore *single-lasted* shoes, which means**

   a. shoes were kept on with a single strip of elastic instead of laces.

   b. shoes could be switched from one foot to the other, so they took longer to wear out.

   c. shoes could be worn only once—but they were very cheap to make.

3. **True or false? Girls in Felicity's time didn't wear underpants.**

4. **Felicity first saw the gown of her dreams on**

   a. Annabelle.

   b. Lady Dunmore.

   c. a fashion doll.

5. **When Felicity snuck out at night to ride Penny, she borrowed Ben's**

   a. breeches.

   b. boots.

   c. cape.

Josefina

1. **What did Josefina often wear to shade her face and protect it from the sun? To find out, change each letter to the one that comes after it in the alphabet:**

   QDANYN

2. **True or false? On her feet, Josefina usually wore sandals.**

3. **Tía Dolores taught Josefina many skills. What was one skill she did *not* teach Josefina?**

   a. how to sew herself a fancy dress

   b. how to repair the colcha stitching on Mamá's altar cloth

   c. how to play piano

   d. how to weave blankets

   e. how to read

4. **Match the Spanish word for each clothing item to the English definition.**

   sarape   blouse

   camisa   lacy shawl

   rebozo   warm poncho

   mantilla   long scarf or shawl

Addy

1. **The night Addy escaped from the plantation, what did she wear?**
    a. as many clothes as she could put on, since she couldn't take a suitcase
    b. a Confederate soldier's uniform
    c. boys' clothing

2. **True or false? In Addy's time, underpants were called *drawers*.**

3. **What did Mrs. Ford give Addy so she could practice her sewing?**
    a. a sampler
    b. an apron
    c. an elegant dress

4. **What did Addy's friend Sarah use to patch the holes in her shoes?**
    a. newspaper
    b. fabric scraps
    c. cardboard
    d. waxed paper

5. **The hair net Addy used to keep her hair in place was known as a _____. To find out the name, change each letter to the one that comes before it in the alphabet:**

    T O P P E

Samantha

1. In 1904, people wore special clothing to go for a drive in an automobile. Which of these items would they *not* have worn for driving?

    a. pattens

    b. goggles

    c. a duster

    d. a hat tied on with a veil

2. Grandmary didn't want Samantha to go driving with Uncle Gard because she was afraid that Samantha would

    a. get hurt.

    b. be frightened.

    c. ruin her clothes.

    d. lose her hat.

3. One of Grandmary's rules was "long underwear from September to the end of _____."

    a. March   c. May

    b. April   d. June

4. Admiral Beemis gave Samantha, Agnes, and Agatha _____ hats. Fill in the blank by unscrambling the letters:

    RILOSA

Kit

1. True or false? For Christmas, Ruthie gave Kit her old Christmas dress from last year.

2. Mother's Christmas gift to Kit was

   a. a new coat, hat, and mittens.

   b. a black Scottie dog pin.

   c. a scarf knit from the wool of an old sweater.

   d. tea at Shillito's Department Store.

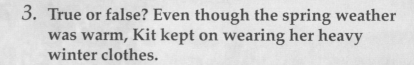

3. True or false? Even though the spring weather was warm, Kit kept on wearing her heavy winter clothes.

4. Aunt Millie made Kit a dress out of

   a. a worn-out sheet.

   b. one of Mother's old dresses.

   c. a chicken-feed sack.

   d. Dad's old coat.

5. What did Kit, Stirling, and Ruthie collect for the children at the soup kitchen? Unscramble the words to find out:

   STACO DAN HOSES

Molly

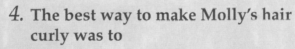

1. Emily and Molly dressed alike
in blue skirts and sweaters,
white blouses, and blue knee socks
because that was their

    a. navy nurse outfit.

    b. princess outfit.

    c. prep school outfit.

2. To buy a home permanent kit,
Molly, Linda, and Susan used

    a. their movie money.

    b. their allowance.

    c. money they had earned by
collecting scrap metal.

3. True or false? Susan gave Molly a home permanent.

4. The best way to make Molly's hair
curly was to

    a. use a home permanent kit.

    b. roll her hair around juice cans.

    c. pin her wet hair in curls.

5. When Emily said the English word *plimsolls*,
Molly knew she meant

    a. roller skates.

    b. rubber boots.

    c. sneakers.

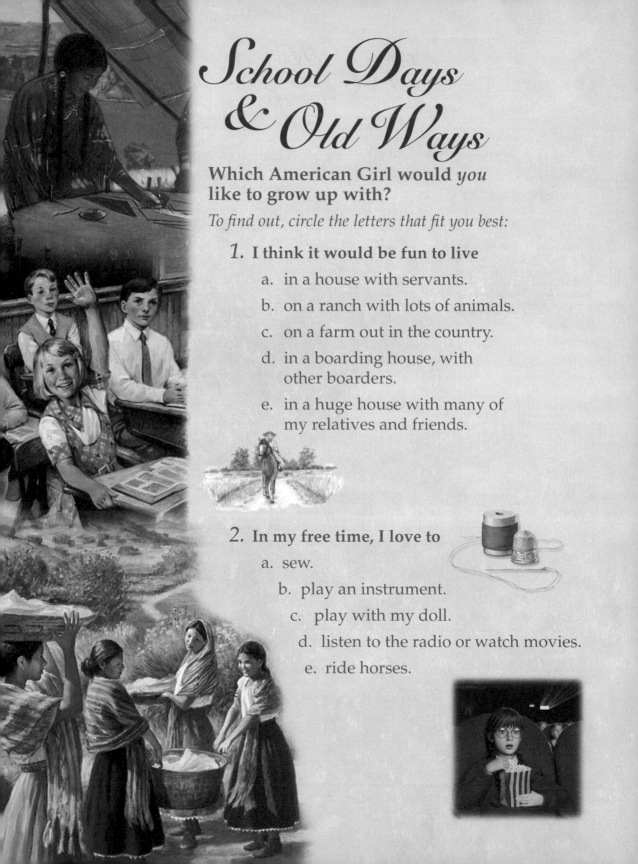

School Days & Old Ways

Which American Girl would *you* like to grow up with?

To find out, circle the letters that fit you best:

1. **I think it would be fun to live**

    a. in a house with servants.

    b. on a ranch with lots of animals.

    c. on a farm out in the country.

    d. in a boarding house, with other boarders.

    e. in a huge house with many of my relatives and friends.

2. **In my free time, I love to**

    a. sew.

    b. play an instrument.

    c. play with my doll.

    d. listen to the radio or watch movies.

    e. ride horses.

3. **For school, I would like**

    a. having lessons at a small private academy.

    b. being home-schooled.

    c. going to a one-room schoolhouse.

    d. attending a public school.

    e. not going to school at all!

4. **The hardest thing for me to live without would be**

    a. a telephone.

    b. music.

    c. animals.

    d. a car.

    e. lots of fresh air and exercise.

Scoring

Mostly a's

You'd fit in with Felicity or Samantha. Although they lived in different times, their lives were similar in some respects—their families had servants, they attended small private schools, and they both had to sew samplers. One difference—Samantha's home had a telephone!

Mostly b's

You'd feel right at home with Josefina, whose family raised sheep and goats on their rancho. Josefina loved playing the piano and listening to Papá play the violin. She was schooled at home, first by Mamá and then by Tía Dolores, who taught her to play the piano.

Mostly c's

You'd like life on the farm with Kirsten. There weren't many neighbors close by, but there were plenty of farm animals to enjoy—including Caro the dog, Blackie the horse, and Missy the cat, who had kittens! When Kirsten wasn't busy with school or chores, she loved creating special places and foods for her doll.

Mostly d's

You'd be happy in Kit's or Molly's world, and just maybe in Addy's, too. All three girls attended public schools, and Addy and Kit both lived in boarding houses. In the 1930s and '40s, you could listen to the radio and watch movies, just like Kit and Molly. But in Addy's time, you'd have to do without radio, movies, and cars!

Mostly e's

You would click with Kaya. In the winter, her family lived in a longhouse with many other families. Kaya didn't go to school. Instead, she spent most days doing outdoor activities, such as helping to gather food or riding her horse, Steps High.

Test your American Girl expertise!
Can you match each girl to her school description?

Kaya

Kirsten

Samantha

Felicity

Addy

Molly

A.
My class studies world geography and current events, followed by multiplication (yuck!). Sometimes we start the day with patriotic songs.

B.
At my school, I study French, natural sciences, penmanship, and *calisthenics,* or exercises. Only girls go to my school.

C.
For a proper education as a gentlewoman, I must learn to sew fancy stitches, dance, and serve tea. It's really quite pleasant!

D.
I start the school day with review of the alphabet. Then it's on to spelling, followed by lessons on *piety,* or good behavior.

F.
For me, education means learning how to gentle a horse, paint hides, weave baskets, and dry salmon.

E.
Our teacher has us recite long poems from memory. We even recite our arithmetic out loud, all of us together. Sometimes our class can be heard from half a mile away!

Kaya

1. Kaya's people built *cairns*, or stone piles, to mark sacred places. When Kaya built a cairn, she wanted to leave something of her own on it, so she took a feather she'd collected and set it on top. What kind of feather was it? (Hint: Think of Kaya's nickname!)

    a. hawk

    b. magpie

    c. swan

    d. eagle

2. When Kaya and her family traveled, they often carried *pemmican* to eat. Pemmican was a tasty, nourishing food made of

    a. fresh salmon and herbs.

    b. sweet, tender roots.

    c. dried meat and berries.

3. Kaya learned about the past from her elders. Her grandmother Aalah told the story of how Nez Perces traded with other tribes at the Big River. The other tribes brought with them goods from pale-faced strangers—and also _____. For the answer, unscramble the word:

    S K I N S E C S

4. **Match these Nez Perce words with their meanings:**

tawts	the people
aa-heh	mother
Nimíipuu	thank you
Hun-ya-wat	guardian spirit
wyakin	good
Eetsa	the creator
Toe-ta	yes
katsee-yow-yow	father

5. **Kaya and her friends liked to play a stickball game called Shinny, in which two teams chased a rawhide ball down an open field, hitting the ball with curved sticks. This game is similar to what sport played by girls today?**

a. lacrosse

b. softball

c. field hockey

d. soccer

Kirsten

1. **True or false? The one-room schoolhouse Kirsten attended was called Powderhorn School.**

2. **At first Kirsten didn't like school because**
    a. she hated being indoors.
    b. she couldn't read English.
    c. other students were mean.
    d. the teacher was mean.

3. **True or false? Kirsten and her classmates didn't use notebooks or paper in school.**

4. **True or false? In Kirsten's day, if a teacher came to live with your family, it was considered a punishment.**

5. **Kirsten didn't want Miss Winston to live with Uncle Olav's family, because she was afraid Miss Winston would**
    a. smack her ruler on Uncle Olav's table.
    b. assign extra homework on the weekends.
    c. look down on the Larsons' Swedish traditions.

Addy

1. **At school, Addy sat next to Harriet. Harriet was named after Harriet Tubman, who helped run the Underground Railroad. That was**

    a. a train station in North Carolina.

    b. the routes and safe houses that slaves used to escape to the North.

    c. a series of caves and tunnels in the mountains of Pennsylvania.

2. **When Addy was teaching Momma how to read, what did Addy use to make letters? Unscramble the words to find out.**

    O K I O C E   H O G U D

3. **These are the words Addy, Sarah, and Harriet had to spell in the spelling match. Are any of them misspelled?**

    carriage   button   tomorow   acount

    bridge   scissors   prinsiple

4. **Addy won the spelling match, but she still felt sad. Why?**

    a. Because she knew she had hurt Sarah.

    b. Because she knew Harriet would be angry about losing.

    c. Because she realized she could spell better than her mother.

Samantha

1. When Miss Stevens asked what *la gorge* meant, Samantha knew that it was French for

    a. canyon.   b. beauty.   c. throat.   d. filled up.

2. True or false? The boys at school called Samantha "dummy" and "ragbag."

3. What was the subject of the speaking contest?
    a. Factory safety
    b. Progress in America
    c. Child labor

4. Nellie told Samantha what working in a thread factory was really like. Nellie worked six days a week, from seven in the morning until seven at night. She had to stand all day in bare feet, and there was no heat in the winter. What was her pay for one week of work?
    a. $1.80   b. $6.00   c. $10.00

5. What did Samantha and Nellie call their school? Unscramble the words to find out.

    NUMOT   TREBET   LOSHOC

Molly

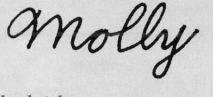

1. What did Molly absolutely hate at school?

    a. gym class

    b. her teacher

    c. multiplication bees

    d. the old gum stuck under her desk

2. True or false? In the multiplication bee, Molly did not know the answer to 8 x 7.

3. What did the boys in Molly's class decide to collect for the Lend-A-Hand contest?

    a. tinfoil

    b. scrap metal

    c. bottle tops

4. What did Molly, Linda, and Susan call themselves when they came up with a secret plan to win the Lend-A-Hand contest? To find out, change each letter to the one before it in the alphabet:

    U P Q   T F D S F U   B H F O U T

5. True or false? The third-grade girls won the school Lend-A-Hand contest by knitting socks.

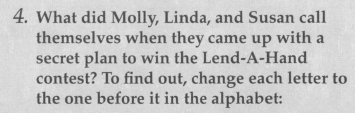

Furry & Feathered Friends

American girls have always had a special bond with animals!

1. **Do you have any pets at home? If so, list them here:**

   Type of Animal   *Name*

2. **If you could have any pet, what kind would you choose?**

3. **Draw a picture of your favorite pet—or a pet you'd like to have.**

4. Match the American Girls to their animal friends!

Kaya

Kirsten

Josefina

Kit

Samantha

Molly

Addy

Felicity

Kaya

1. **True or false? Kaya's dog was called Lone Dog.**

2. **Kaya named Lone Dog's largest puppy Tatlo because he reminded her of**

   a. a gray wolf.

   b. a cute baby.

   c. a ground squirrel.

   d. a bright-eyed blue jay.

3. **What kind of horse was Steps High? To find out, unscramble the word:**

   LOSAPOAPA

4. **Steps High was 13 hands high at the shoulder. That's the same as**

   a. 52 inches.   c. 52 centimeters.

   b. 4 feet, 4 inches.   d. a and b.

5. **In *Meet Kaya*, two boys challenged Kaya to a horserace. How did the race end?**

   a. Kaya and Steps High left the boys in the dust!

   b. Toe-ta caught Kaya and the boys and ordered them to stop!

   c. Steps High suddenly began to buck and didn't finish the race!

6. **More than a year after Steps High was stolen by raiders, Kaya found her again—with a foal at her side! But Kaya had to rescue the horses from a terrible danger. What was it?**

    a. an earthquake

    b. a forest fire

    c. a flood

    d. an avalanche

7. **Help Kaya find Steps High! Her mare had a distinctive blaze, or white mark, on her face. Which one is it?**

a

b

c

d

Felicity

1. True or false? Felicity named Jiggy Nye's horse Penny because he kept her in a pen.

2. When Felicity visited Penny, she always brought
   a. an apple.
   b. a lump of sugar.
   c. a carrot.
   d. a handful of oats.

3. Ben said Penny was a "blood horse," which meant she was trained to be a
   a. racehorse.
   b. war horse.
   c. gentleman's mount.

4. True or false? In *Meet Felicity*, Felicity rode Penny in a sidesaddle.

5. What pet did Grandfather bring for Felicity, Nan, and William?
   a. a pony
   b. a lamb
   c. a puppy

6. What did Felicity name the pet Grandfather brought? (Hint: It's an old-fashioned word for flower.)

Josefina

1. True or false? Josefina's favorite goat was named Florecita.

2. What did Florecita especially like to eat?
    a. tortillas
    b. flowers
    c. shoes
    d. bizcochitos

3. True or false? Florecita died giving birth.

4. Josefina named the baby goat Sombrita. In Spanish, that means
    a. pretty girl.
    b. little shadow.
    c. funny hat.

5. Josefina saved Sombrita's life by
    a. letting the goat suck milk off of her fingers.
    b. pulling Sombrita out of a fast-flowing stream.
    c. throwing a rock at a rattlesnake.
    d. a and c.

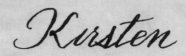

Kirsten

1. **When Missy the cat had kittens, which kitten was Kirsten's favorite?**

    a. the biggest one

    b. the prettiest one

    c. the weakest one

2. **What was the name of the Larsons' horse?**

    a. Blackie   b. Brownie   c. Whitey

3. **True or false? Kirsten was a good horseback rider.**

4. **When Kirsten and Peter took Caro fishing with them, the puppy dashed out of the woods yelping with pain. Why?**

    a. He got his paw caught in a trap.

    b. He was stung by a bee.

    c. He was bitten by a rattlesnake.

    d. He was clawed by a bear.

5. **When Kirsten, Lars, and John walked the trap line, what did they find caught in the last trap? Unscramble the words to find out.**

    A B B Y   C R O N O C A

6. **"You can't make a pet out of a wild animal, Kirsten," Lars told her. But Kirsten proved Lars wrong. True or false?**

Kit

1. True or false? Kit adored Uncle Hendrick's little dog, Inky.

2. Aunt Millie decided that the Kittredges should keep _____ in their backyard. For the answer, change each letter to the one that comes before it in the alphabet:

   D I J D L F O T

3. Kit found a pitiful, starving dog in the street. The dog was abandoned, so Kit brought it home. What kind of dog was it?

   a. a hound

   b. a terrier

   c. a collie

   d. a spaniel

4. Mother said, "Well, I hope you're happy, dog. It's thanks to you that my garden club party was the party to end all parties." Why did Mother say this?

   a. The dog had puppies right in the middle of the party!

   b. Kit had taught the dog clever tricks that amazed the garden club ladies!

   c. The dog chased the chickens into the dining room, where the ladies were having lunch!

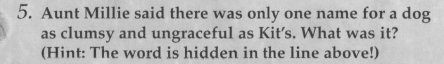

5. Aunt Millie said there was only one name for a dog as clumsy and ungraceful as Kit's. What was it? (Hint: The word is hidden in the line above!)

Tough Times

The American Girls had many hardships, from natural disasters to best-friend feuds.

Can you name the girls who faced these challenges? The first one has been done for you.

1. Water and fire

Samantha rowed across a lake in a rainstorm in the middle of the night.

_____'s family lost most of their sheep in a flash flood.

_____ rescued her mother from drowning in a river they were crossing.

_____ was trapped in a gulch, surrounded by fire, with only one way out—straight up the cliff!

2. Fashion disasters

_____ had to wear her older brother's clumsy, heavy rubber boots when she outgrew her own rainboots.

_____ was supposed to wear hot, itchy wool stockings from September to June.

_____ didn't want to wear her old brown dress to the dancing lesson at the Governor's Palace.

_____ caught a cold from sleeping in wet pin curls each night.

Molly comforted Emily during a blackout.

3. Best friends

_____ hurt the feelings of her good friend _____ when she chose to spend time after school with the popular girls instead of her friend.

_____ and _____ argued about what kind of birthday party they should have.

_____ was too proud to wear her best friend _____'s hand-me-down dress at Christmastime.

_____ was afraid _____ would no longer speak to her after her friend's father was thrown in jail.

4. Breaking rules

_____ helped her friends sneak out of an orphanage.

_____ went out secretly each night, wearing boys' breeches, to visit her favorite animal.

_____ skipped a whole day of school to play with her secret friend.

_____ hopped a freight train, just because she wanted an adventure!

Kaya

1. Kaya was ashamed of her nickname. What was it? To find out, change each letter to the one that comes before it in the alphabet:

   N B H Q J F

2. Kaya's grandmother Kautsa told Kaya the story of the nickname she had been called as a child. Unscramble the words to find out what it was. (Hint: The nickname was a kind of food Kaya liked!)

   G R I N E F   S E A C K

3. Before she died, Swan Circling gave Kaya several important gifts. Which of the following items was *not* a gift that Swan Circling gave to Kaya?

   a. digging stick   c. a new name

   b. a saddle   d. confidence in herself

4. True or false? Kaya's sister, Speaking Rain, was deaf.

5. Kaya and Speaking Rain were captured by raiders and stolen from their village. Who were the raiders?

   a. Salish Indians

   b. enemies from Buffalo Country

   c. white people moving into the territory

6. True or false? When Kaya escaped the raiders' village in the middle of the night, she left Speaking Rain behind.

Josefina

1. Josefina was afraid of lightning, and Mamá wasn't there to comfort her in the storm. Who gave Josefina the courage to face the storm?

    a. Papá

    b. Tía Dolores

    c. Tía Magdalena

2. Josefina wanted something that Abuelito's caravan could not bring her—something that would help her stand up to Florecita! What was it? Add the missing vowels to find out.

    C _ _ R _ G _

3. Josefina missed Mamá very much. To keep Mamá's memory alive, she

    a. played Mamá's favorite song on the violin.

    b. wove blankets on Mamá's loom.

    c. watered Mamá's flowers.

    d. a and b.

4. True or false? Francisca didn't want to learn to read and write, because she thought it would make her forget Mamá.

5. Josefina was brokenhearted that Tía Dolores was leaving the rancho. What did Tía Magdalena give Josefina to keep her hope alive?

    a. a heart milagro

    b. a little book of Mamá's prayers, poems, and sayings

    c. a branch of apricot blossoms

Addy

1. **What crop was grown on the plantation where Addy's family was enslaved? Unscramble the word to find out:**

BOCATOC

2. **In Addy's time, soldiers fighting for the South wore gray uniforms and were called Confederate soldiers. Those fighting for the North wore blue uniforms and were called _____ soldiers.**

    a. Rebel   b. Loyalist   c. Patriot   d. Union

3. **When Addy decided to give her money to the Freedmen's Fund, she remembered these words from Uncle Solomon:**

    a. "Freedom's got its cost."

    b. "A penny saved is a penny earned."

    c. "The Lord helps those who help themselves."

4. **True or false? It would take Momma more than two months to earn $10.00 working in Mrs. Ford's shop.**

5. **In Philadelphia, Poppa had a job delivering**

    a. milk.

    b. ice.

    c. ice cream.

Samantha

1. **True or false? Miss Frouchy was kind and generous.**

2. **When Samantha went to visit Nellie at Coldrock House, which of these did Miss Frouchy *not* say?**

    a. Gifts spoil girls and make them selfish.

    b. Orphan girls must be grateful to their betters.

    c. The rules are: Obedience. Order. Discipline.

    d. Cleanliness is next to godliness.

3. **When Samantha went to Teardrop Island with Agnes and Agatha, lots of things went wrong. Can you put these events in order?**

    A. It began to rain.

    B. The admiral hit his head on a rock.

    C. Samantha lost her balance and almost toppled into the water.

    D. The girls forgot to tie up the canoe.

    E. They heard a rustling noise coming closer and closer.

    F. The rowboat got caught between two rocks, and Samantha had to free it.

    G. When they got back to the beach, the canoe was missing.

4. **Admiral Beemis gave Samantha a gift that turned out to be very helpful in the rescue. What was it?**

    a. a special canoe paddle

    b. a butterfly net

    c. a bo's'n's whistle

Kit

1. Kit's father lost his business in the Depression. What kind of business was it?

    a. a car dealership

    b. an insurance company

    c. a family diner

2. With Dad out of work, the Kittredges' biggest fear was that they would l _ s _   t h _ _ r   h _ _ s_. To find out what it was, add the missing vowels!

3. With Dad out of a job, Mother had a brainstorm. What was it?

    a. to have a garden party

    b. to raise chickens and sell the eggs

    c. to open a boarding house

    d. to move in with Uncle Hendrick

4. True or false? As part of her dusting chores, Kit skated down the hall in socks and slid down the banister.

5. **When Kit saw Dad at the _____ _____, she realized how poor her family really was.**

   a. welfare office

      b. soup kitchen

         c. hobo jungle

6. **True or false? After visiting the hobo jungle, Kit realized that hobo life might be fun, sort of like camping.**

7. **Uncle Hendrick came to stay at Kit's house because he had a _____ _____ _____ ____. To fill in the blanks, unscramble the words:**

   N O B E R K   K A L E N   D A N   S W T I R

8. **Draw lines to connect Uncle Hendrick and Aunt Millie to their opinions:**

Aunt Millie

Uncle Hendrick

   a. Children and seeds are never disappointing.

   b. Hope never put a nickel in anybody's pocket.

   c. Hobos are thieves and beggars.

   d. A nickel and some friendliness works every time.

Food, Fun & Games

Throughout history, girls have always been expert at having fun!

1. **If you were having a party and could pick one of these games to play with your guests, which one would you pick?**

   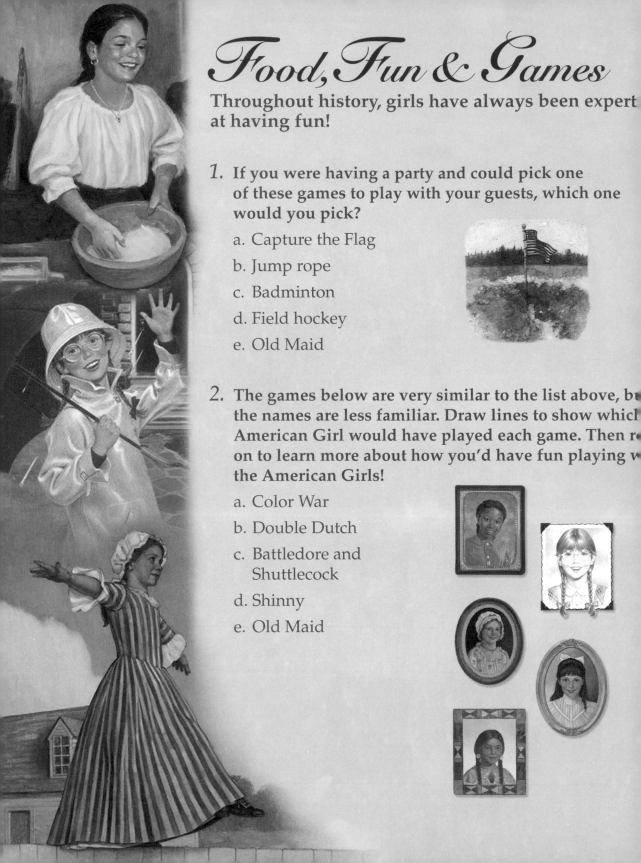

   a. Capture the Flag

   b. Jump rope

   c. Badminton

   d. Field hockey

   e. Old Maid

2. **The games below are very similar to the list above, bu the names are less familiar. Draw lines to show which American Girl would have played each game. Then r on to learn more about how you'd have fun playing w the American Girls!**

   a. Color War

   b. Double Dutch

   c. Battledore and Shuttlecock

   d. Shinny

   e. Old Maid

For your party game, if you picked . . .

a, you'd have good times with Molly. The Color War at Camp Gowonagin was an elaborate game of Capture the Flag. You'd want a lot of girls at your party for this game!

b, Addy would be a good guest to invite! By listening to the rhythm of the jump ropes slapping the sidewalk, Addy finally learned to jump Double Dutch. Can you?

c, Felicity would fit right in at your party. The old English game of Battledore and Shuttlecock was popular in the American colonies in the 1700s.

d, Kaya's your girl. Shinny was also played by Indians and Spanish settlers in Josefina's time. It's still played today on some Indian reservations.

e, you'd want to invite Samantha—and Agnes and Agatha, too! They played Old Maid with the Admiral at Piney Point. The game was brand-new back in 1904, and it's still popular today.

3. **Test your American Girls expertise! Which American Girl would be most likely to eat each of these foods?**

_____ tortillas and bizcochitos

_____ Boston brown bread with no sugar or butter

_____ biscuits and queen cakes with tea

_____ roasted fish and finger cakes

_____ sweet potato pudding

_____ soup made from bones and meat scraps

Josefina

1. Josefina loved spreading adobe plaster on the walls of the church with her bare hands. What was the adobe plaster made of? Unscramble the words to find out.

   U M D   E T W R A   W R S A T

2. Josefina and her sisters baked bread in a special kind of outdoor oven called a

   a. pueblo.   c. horno.

   b. rebozo.   d. milagro.

3. At the market in Santa Fe, Josefina and her sisters could each choose one thing they wanted to trade for. Match each sister with the item she wanted.

Ana	mirror
Francisca	toy farm
Clara	boots
Josefina	knitting needles

4. That night in Santa Fe, when Josefina heard Papá's music, she knew exactly what she wanted to trade her blanket for. What was it?

   a. sheet music   b. Patrick's violin   c. a piano

5. Francisca joked that Josefina's hopes were like something that always rose, no matter how much you flattened it. What was that something? Unscramble the letters to find out.

   D A B E R   U H D G O

Kirsten

1. On Kirsten's first night at Uncle Olav's farm, Anna and Lisbeth promised that they would show Kirsten their _____ _____ the next day. For the answer, unscramble the letters.

   CREEST   ROFT

2. Kirsten, Anna, and Lisbeth liked to make mud cakes for their dolls' lunch. What did they use to decorate the cakes? Add the missing vowels:

   G _ _ S _ B _ RR _ _ S   _ C _ RN C _ PS
   S _ NFL _ W _ R   S _ _ DS

3. True or false? In December, Kirsten's family celebrated a Swedish holiday called Saint Maria's Day.

4. Which of the following was *not* a gift that Singing Bird gave to Kirsten?

   a. a purple bead
   b. a doll cake decorated with shells
   c. a green duck feather
   d. a clay pot the size of an acorn

Samantha

1. What was Samantha's favorite flavor of ice cream? To find out, change each letter to the one that comes after it in the alphabet:

   O D O O D Q L H M S

2. What did Eddie Ryland put in the ice cream at Samantha's birthday?

   a. salt
   b. pepper
   c. sand

3. Which of the following was *not* one of the activities Samantha and Cornelia did together at Christmastime?

   a. sledding
   b. shopping
   c. putting up Christmas decorations
   d. making a gingerbread house
   e. singing Christmas carols

4. True or false? When Samantha ate gingerbread, she always thought of Nellie.

5. What did Samantha and Nellie call the hole in the lilac hedge? Unscramble the words to find out:

   H E T   N E L U N T

Molly

1. Molly told Emily that she had thought Emily would look like the English princess, Elizabeth. Emily grinned and replied, "I rather expected you to look like _____ _____, the film star!" To find out who Emily was thinking of, change each letter to the one that comes before it in the alphabet.

   TIJSMFZ UFNQMF

2. Molly and Emily wanted to have an English tea party for their birthday party, but they had a hard time agreeing on the menu. Which item did Emily say was *not* proper to have at an English tea party?

   a. meat paste sandwiches

   b. bread and butter

   c. lemon tart

   d. treacle pudding

   e. tea with milk

3. True or false? Molly thought Dorinda's plan for capturing the Red Army flag was a good one.

4. During the Color War, what did Molly throw on Linda's head to distract her so that Molly could free the rest of the Blue Army?

   a. a can of worms

   b. underwear

   c. a bucket of water

ANSWERS
Who's Who

Kaya *pages 6–7*

1. SHE WHO ARRANGES ROCKS

2. d

3. b

5. a

4. Kaya's twin brothers — Brown Deer and Speaking Rain
Kaya's sisters — Fox Tail and Raven
Kaya's parents — Steps High and Sparks Flying
two boys who bother Kaya — Toe-ta and Eetsa
Kaya's horse and her foal — Wing Feather and Sparrow

6. dried meat — baby carrier
cattail fluff — teething biscuit
medicine woman — disposable diapers
cradleboard — pediatrician

Felicity *pages 8–9*

1. b

2.

	Patriot	Loyalist
Felicity's father	x	
Grandfather		x
Elizabeth's father		x
Ben	x	

3. Ben — shopkeeper
Father — plantation owner
Miss Manderly — tanner
Isaac — apprentice
Jiggy Nye — teacher
Grandfather — drummer in the militia

4. False. Felicity and Annabelle did not get along.

5. c

6. b

Josefina *pages 10–11*

1. True

2. Josefina — impatient, headstrong
Clara — hopeful, timid
Francisca — gentle, understanding
Ana — practical, sensible

3. True. New Mexico did not become part of the United States until 1846, when Josefina would have been 33 years old.

4. False. She was Papá's sister.

6. c

7. Juan, Antonio

5.

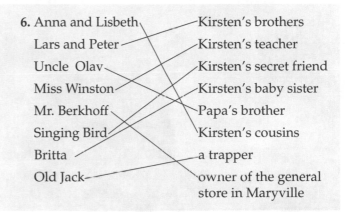

Teresita — Tía Dolores's servant
Abuelito — Josefina's grandfather
Carmen — the cook on the rancho
Patrick O'Toole — an American scout
Mariana — the doll Mamá had made
Niña — the cook's husband
Miguel — Josefina's friend, a Pueblo Indian

Kirsten *pages 12–13*

1. a

2. MINNESOTA

3. b

4. c

5. True. Mormor had said, "When you're lonely, look at the sun. Remember that we all see the same sun."

6.
Anna and Lisbeth — Kirsten's cousins
Lars and Peter — Kirsten's brothers
Uncle Olav — a trapper
Miss Winston — Kirsten's teacher
Mr. Berkhoff — owner of the general store in Maryville
Singing Bird — Kirsten's secret friend
Britta — Kirsten's baby sister
Old Jack — Papa's brother

Addy *pages 14–15*

1. c

2. a

3. True

4. b

6. a skunk

5.
Auntie Lula — the cook on the plantation in North Carolina
Master Stevens — the cruel plantation owner in North Carolina
Sarah — Addy's best friend in Philadelphia
Miss Dunn — owner of a small dress shop in Philadelphia
Mrs. Ford — a lady who runs a safe house on the Underground Railroad
M'dear — Mr. Golden's mother, who lives at the boarding house
Reverend Drake — the preacher at Trinity A.M.E. Church
Miss Caroline — Addy's teacher at Sixth Street School

Samantha *pages 16–17*

1. Uncle Gard — Grandmary's son
   Jenny and Bridget — Cornelia's twin sisters
   Agnes and Agatha — Nellie's little sisters
   Elsa — Grandmary's grouchy maid
   Hawkins — Grandmary's butler
   Grandmary — Samantha's grandmother
   Cornelia — Uncle Gard's lady friend
   Nellie — Samantha's friend, a servant girl

2. True   3. e   4. False. She left to have a baby.   5. d   6. a

Kit *pages 18–19*

1. a   2. False. Kit felt out of place in the frilly room.   3. b   4. a   5. BRAINSTORM

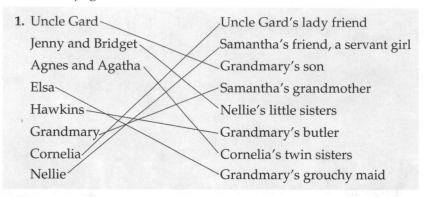

6. Stirling Howard — a boarder at Kit's house
   Ruthie Smithens — Kit's best friend
   Uncle Hendrick — Mother's disapproving uncle
   Will — a hobo
   Gibb — the newspaper editor
   Charlie — Kit's brother
   Aunt Millie — the thrifty woman who raised Dad

Molly *pages 20–21*

1. b   2. c   3. DOCTOR   4. c   5. a

6. Emily Bennett — a girl from England
   Mrs. Gilford — the McIntires' housekeeper
   Miss Campbell — the camp director
   Miss LaVonda — Molly's dance teacher
   Linda and Susan — Molly's good friends
   Elizabeth and Margaret Rose — the English princesses
   Miss Butternut — Molly's third-grade teacher

Fabulous Fashions page 23

5. bloomers   sunbonnet   (sarape)
   breeches   boater   drawers
   (pattens)   mob cap   shift
   pantalettes   (camisa)   underpetticoat

6. bloomers — Molly
   mob cap — Kirsten
   buckskin dress — Felicity
   sarape — Samantha
   feed-sack dress — Josefina
   saddle shoes — Kaya
   sunbonnet — Kit

Felicity *page 24*

1. False. Stays itched and pinched!   2. b   3. True!   4. c   5. a

Josefina *page 25*

1. REBOZO   2. False. She wore moccasins.   3. d

4. sarape — blouse
   camisa — lacy shawl
   rebozo — warm poncho
   mantilla — long scarf or shawl

Addy *page 26*

1. c   2. True   3. b   4. a

5. SNOOD

Samantha *page 27*

1. a   2. c   3. d   4. SAILOR

Kit *page 28*

1. True. But at first Kit would not accept the gift because she was ashamed.

2. b   3. True. She had outgrown her spring clothes from last year.   4. c   5. COATS AND SHOES

Molly *page 29*

1. b   2. a   3. False. Jill stopped them just in time!   4. c   5. c

F. E. B. C. D. A.

Kaya *pages 34–35*

1. b **2.** c

3. SICKNESS

5. c

4. tawts — the creator
aa-heh — yes
Nimíipuu — the people
Hun-ya-wat — the creator
wyakin — guardian spirit
Eetsa — mother
Toe-ta — father
katsee-yow-yow — thank you

(word matching: tawts = good, aa-heh = yes, Nimíipuu = the people, Hun-ya-wat = the creator, wyakin = guardian spirit, Eetsa = mother, Toe-ta = father, katsee-yow-yow = thank you)

Kirsten *page 36*

1. False. It was called Powderkeg School.

2. b

3. True. They wrote their lessons on slates and recited them out loud in class.

4. False. It was considered an honor.

5. a

Addy *page 37*

1. b **2.** COOKIE DOUGH **3.** tomorrow, account, principle **4.** a

Samantha *page 38*

1. c **2.** False. That was what they called Nellie.

3. b **4.** b **5.** MOUNT BETTER SCHOOL

Molly *page 39*

1. c **2.** True **3.** a **4.** TOP SECRET AGENTS

5. False. They knitted a blanket.

4.

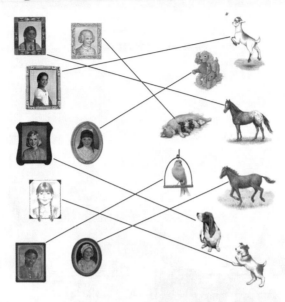

Kaya *pages 42–43*

1. False. Lone Dog was wild. Her puppy, Tatlo, became Kaya's dog.

2. c   **3.** APPALOOSA   **4.** d   **5.** c   **6.** b   **7.**

d

Felicity *page 44*

1. False. Felicity thought the horse was the color of a   **2.** a   **3.** c
bright copper penny—and also that she was inde*pen*dent!

4. False. She rode Penny bareback.   **5.** b   **6.** Posie

Josefina *page 45*

1. False. Josefina was afraid of Florecita   **2.** b   **3.** True   **4.** b   **5.** d
and thought she was mean!

Kirsten *page 46*

1. c   **2.** a   **3.** True. She rode Blackie at a fast gallop to fetch Aunt Inger
when Mama was having her baby!

4. b   **5.** BABY RACCOON   **6.** False. Lars was right—the raccoon caused
a fire that burned down the house!

Kit *page 47*

1. False. Kit thought Inky was
the meanest, most hateful
dog in Cincinnati.

2. CHICKENS   **3.** a

4. c   **5.** Grace

67

Tough Times *pages 48–49*

1. Samanatha
   Josefina
   Addy
   Kaya

2. Molly
   Samantha
   Felicity
   Molly

3. Addy, Sarah
   Molly, Emily
   Kit, Ruthie
   Felicity, Elizabeth

4. Samantha
   Felicity
   Kirsten
   Kit

Kaya *page 50*

1. MAGPIE   **2.** FINGER CAKES   **3.** a   **4.** False. She was blind.   **5.** b   **6.** True

Josefina *page 51*

1. b   **2.** COURAGE   **3.** c   **4.** True   **5.** a

Addy *page 52*

1. TOBACCO   **2.** d   **3.** a   **4.** True   **5.** b

Samantha *page 53*

1. False. Miss Frouchy was mean and stingy.   **2.** d   **3.** D, G, A, E, B, F, C   **4.** c

Kit *pages 54–55*

1. a
2. lose their house
3. c
4. True
5. b
6. False. She realized hobo life was very hard.
7. BROKEN ANKLE AND WRIST

8.

   a. Children and seeds are never disappointing.
   b. Hope never put a nickel in anybody's pocket.
   c. Hobos are thieves and beggars.
   d. A nickel and some friendliness works every time.

2.
a. Color War
b. Double Dutch
c. Battledore and Shuttlecock
d. Shinny
e. Old Maid

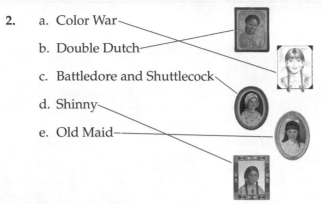

3. <u>Josefina</u>   tortillas and bizcochitos

    <u>Molly</u>   Boston brown bread with no sugar or butter

    <u>Felicity</u>   biscuits and queen cakes with tea

    <u>Kaya</u>   roasted fish and finger cakes

    <u>Addy</u>   sweet potato pudding

    <u>Kit</u>   soup made from bones and meat scraps

Josefina *page 58*

1. MUD, WATER, STRAW   **2.** c

4. b

5. BREAD DOUGH

3. Ana — mirror
Francisca — toy farm
Clara — boots
Josefina — knitting needles

Kirsten *page 59*

1. SECRET FORT

2. GOOSEBERRIES, ACORN CAPS, SUNFLOWER SEEDS

3. False. The holiday was called Saint Lucia's Day.

4. b

Samantha *page 60*

1. PEPPERMINT   **2.** a   **3.** c   **4.** True   **5.** THE TUNNEL

Molly *page 61*

1. SHIRLEY TEMPLE   **2.** d   **3.** False. Molly thought the plan would fail.   **4.** a